Wandering Woman: Nevada

The Ultimate Road Trip: One Woman's
Journey Across the United States by Car

Julie Bettendorf

Contents

Introduction

"Not all who wander are lost."

Are you sure? I thought to myself, as I tried not to panic. I was a long way from anything familiar, but that was how it should be. I had driven thousands of miles on dusty, pothole-filled roads. It's often on the worst roads that you can discover something truly amazing.

My dusty CRV was parked beside me, containing one restless dog and a variety of snack bags, all empty by now. There were no buildings in sight, no cars or people or movement at all. Only the constant humming of the insects as they buzzed around my head.

I turned to my left – another straight road that trailed off into the distance. I glanced over to the right, then behind me – two more barely discernible roads stretched out into the abyss. I was in a four-way intersection with no signs, no sense of direction, and no sign of life for several miles. No cell service either, and that meant no GPS. *Damn*, I thought. *I'm lost.*

How did I get here? I couldn't help but feel like this little intersection was a cruel metaphor for life. I began to daydream, imagining each road might transport me back to a different time, a different role in my life, and a different me.

If I took the road from whence I came, it could lead me all the way back to Oregon, back to my cheating third husband, back to a life of loneliness and solitude. There is no greater loneliness than being married to someone who isn't actually present in your life.

If I took the road to my left, perhaps it could take me back to my career as a dental hygienist, a job I hated deep down in my soul. There is something so disengaging about cleaning teeth for a living. It's a disgusting, smelly way to get a paycheck. It pays well, which is great, but the best part is the huge gob of friends I enjoy to this day.

Or maybe the road to my right, *yes – maybe that's the path*, I imagined. Maybe it could take me back to my real treasure, my kids. Back to their smiling, innocent faces as toddlers, as they danced around the Christmas tree and their father and I were still married. Back when they still needed me for every little thing.

But, that was just it. I didn't feel needed anymore. My kids weren't toddlers anymore – they were both full-grown adults, and far too busy for me. My dental buddies were still working, but I wasn't. Dental hygiene had robbed me of the cartilage in my fingers, giving me severe, disabling arthritis. And, I wouldn't be returning to any more husbands either, because three marriages were quite enough for me.

All three of these paths, all three of these roles – the wife, the mother, and the dental hygienist – had seemingly been stripped from me within a year. I was lost and looking to find myself again.

The funny thing about this phrase, "not all who wander are lost" – is that, in my experience, wandering and being lost walk hand-in-hand with one another, and the expression can be flipped. In my experience, not all who are lost are wandering, and that is a real disservice to the beauty and clarity that the world has to offer.

When one becomes lost, wandering is the only option to guide oneself back to a path. After all, one could not come upon any dirt path at all without wandering.

I began wandering at an early age, both with my mind and with my feet. At eight years old, I was reading a book about archaeology and dreaming of one day seeing Egypt. I didn't follow a traditional path in high school either, going heavily into foreign languages, in hopes of one day using them.

At twenty-five years old, I divorced my first husband (the dental student who talked me into becoming a dental hygienist so I could work for him) and decided to give traveling a real shot. I took off for the Andes and Macchu Picchu, climbing up ancient Inca stone steps to reach the magnificent ruins.

Anyone who has been to Macchu Picchu will tell you there is something ethereal and deeply spiritual about the place. The ruins stretch out across the emerald green mountains, way up in the middle of the sky. Macchu Picchu gave me my first experience of feeling history. This trip inspired me to come back and complete a degree in archaeology, and I've been wandering ever since.

More travel followed including a backpack trip around Europe for three months, by myself, and trips to Britain, Italy, and Greece. I visited the burial places of Crusaders, mummies, and ancient kings. I happened upon the castle of my namesake in Bettendorf, Luxembourg, and wandered my way through European history.

My favorite excursion by far was finally seeing Egypt with my daughter in 2012. Just like my childhood dream envisioned, I rode a camel beneath the pyramids of Giza, with my head wrapped in some man's sweaty turban. It was perfect.

Traveling has always been my own personal antidote to pain. I went to Mexico after my first and second divorces, Canada after my third, and Italy after my dad died. Call it avoidance if you want, but I call it an accelerated form of healing in the purest sense of the word. I believe travel can heal your soul.

Wandering has always worked its wonders on me – made me feel renewed, rejoiceful, grateful, and purposeful. It's been my medicine.

So, as I stood in that intersection, I once again wondered how wandering had led me so astray this time. *What the hell am I supposed to do now?* It was then that I realized that one last path had not been considered yet – the path which stretched straight out in front of me. *Which role does this represent?* I pondered.

The answer smacked me in the face.

That last dirt road – the only path that could take me where I wanted to go, the only path that ever truly healed me or showed me the way – was the path of the traveler. The wife, the mother, and the hygienist roles – though valued in their time – were sitting in the bleachers now. It was time to welcome and enable my boldest, bravest, and perhaps most pivotal role yet:

The role of the Wandering Woman.

Welcome to Wandering Woman

This book is for you – the grieving empty nester mom, the begrudged housewife, the woman in need of a drastic change in her life. Really, this book is for anyone with a passion for traveling. If you feel lost with no sense of direction or purpose in life, that's a bonus – this book will be even more appealing to you. And lastly, if you're a man reading this book, congratulations for holding a book with the word woman in the title. You're contributing to gender equality, and that's pretty neat.

I decided to combine three of my dearest loves – travel, history, and archaeology – and put them into a book because I believe wandering has the power to change your life. I have been to many areas of the world and had too many outstanding experiences to list. However, by the time both my children had moved out in 2017, I had never

Me

seen my own country – America. It was the perfect time to explore a new country (my own) and discover a new me at the same time.

So, I packed up my Honda CRV, along with some gear and my 14-year-old furry friend, Sadie. ***Wandering Woman*** is the chronicle of my journey across eleven states, discovering the joy of getting lost and finding myself along the way.

Why America?

A merica, the beautiful? I sure think so, but I didn't realize just how beautiful our country is until I embarked on traveling across eleven western states in a year.

The United States offers everything for the discerning palate. From spectacular beaches, austere mountains, to rolling plains, our country has it all. It's difficult to comprehend just how large and impressive our scenery is, until you experience it first-hand, with the ultimate road trip.

I also realized just how much of our history is missing from U.S. history I was taught as a kid. The history of our country didn't begin with the pilgrims landing on Plymouth Rock in the 1600s. Our history is far more ancient, with rock art and archaeological sites dating back over 12,000 years.

We also owe a tremendous debt to early pioneers who tamed our land. The Mormons and other groups ventured into the great unknown with their families and their worldly possessions. Some of them pulled cumbersome handcarts across the country to settle in inhospitable, dangerous locations.

The goal of Wandering Woman is to bring history back to life and make it interesting again. I am presenting some famous sites, and many little-known ones. You will take the road-less-traveled with me, while we explore ghost towns, rock art sites, archaeological sites, and museums, to discover the colorful tapestry that is our country.

I present some history, including dates, but my goal is to present more of the real-life stories of history, including ghost stories, profiles in history, voices from the past, and moments in time, to give you, the reader, a deeper understanding of the context of history.

This is by no means an exhaustive list of places to visit. In fact, I encourage you to discover America for yourself, as I did, by making a trek across the land by car. You can explore as the early explorers did, just a little more comfortably, with a lot less hardship.

I hope you enjoy this book and take a little time out to discover our beautiful country, and maybe even discover yourself in the process.

Safe Travels,

Julie Bettendorf

Welcome to
Nevada

The Silver State

*N*evada is a surprising state. You can find the desert, and you can find the mountains, and you can find a state that is starkly beautiful. You can find friendly, relaxed Nevadans along with bustling tourism. You can find yourself getting lost in Nevada just for the fun of it.

5 things to love about Nevada:

The early Mormon pioneering history from places like Genoa

The spectacular lights of the Las Vegas Strip

The old mining history from places like Virginia City

The military history from places like Fort Churchill

The Pony Express history from places like Cold Springs Station

Dreams of Nevada

"Las Vegas looks the way you'd imagine heaven must look at night." – **Chuck Palahniuk**

"Las Vegas is the only place I know where money really talks – it says, GOODBYE." – **Frank Sinatra**

"Nevada has a very dynamic economy, with gambling being the number-one industry, followed closely by blood donorship."– **Dave Barry**

Top Stuff to See in Nevada

Favorite Nevada Historical Sites:

- Virginia City
- Berlin Ghost Town

Favorite Nevada Archeological Sites:

- Valley of Fire
- Grimes Point Archaeological Area

Favorite Nevada Museums:

- Reno Automobile Museum
- Nevada State Museum

When driving through Nevada, be on the lookout for:

Wild horses and burros

Early Nevada

Early Camping in Nevada
(courtesy of Reno Automobile Museum)

Goodsprings Pioneer Saloon

A group of students in early Virginia City
(courtesy of Fourth Ward School)

Northern Nevada

Rainbow Ridge Opal Mine

Denio

I took a little detour to **Denio**, site of the **Rainbow Ridge Opal Mine** and for $100 you can sift through tailing material which is what is left after digging out the banks. Another option: for

$700, you and a carefully-chosen friend can pick through a newly excavated pile of dirt. I picked the cheaper option and had a lot of fun. I found a few cool specimens and had a great experience.

There is also a wonderful little BLM campground nearby with a hot springs pool.

How to get to Denio:

The tiny town of Denio is located just below the border with Oregon, 577.5 miles north of Las Vegas, off of Hwy 95 north.

Western Nevada

Buckland Station

Reno

Reno advertises itself as the "Biggest Little City in the World." And it has grown up in the last few years.

My favorite pick for a bit of history is the **Reno Automobile Museum.** If you haven't been there, put it on your bucket list, even if you don't care about cars. It's Harrah's old collection of vintage autos. Finch

There are also vintage wedding dresses, men's clothes, accessories, but the stars are the cars.

A few of my favorites are the cars owned by John F. Kennedy, James Dean, and Frank Sinatra.

I have a few favorites beginning with an early RV from 1921.

Another favorite is the car that won the 1908 trip from New York to Paris.

This is a great museum with a wonderful presentation.

How to get to the Reno Automobile Museum:

The Reno Automobile Museum is located at 10 South Lake Street in Reno.

Virginia City

***V**irginia City* should be on your bucket list. The town was named by James Finney "Old Virginny" who came from

Virginia. Gold was discovered here in 1859 and became the world famous Comstock Lode.

Virginia City was once known as the "richest town in the world." The huge silver finds around Virginia City helped to fund the Union army in the Civil War.

Silver wealth also flowed into San Francisco, funding the Transcontinental Railroad, and Atlantic telegraph cables.

The area population swelled to 75,000 people by 1875. At its height, Virginia City had an opera house, courthouse, schoolhouse, churches, restaurants, saloons, and a red light district. Samuel Clemens came here to work for the Territorial Enterprise newspaper. He first used his pen name Mark Twain, while in Virginia City.

You can start with the *Silver Terrace Cemetery*. What was once a garden of flowers, trees, and neat paths, is now a rocky, barren landscape, filled with old tombstones and well-worn wrought iron fences.

The first burial here was in 1867. The cemetery has some poignant grave stones of mother and daughter buried together, husbands and wives buried together, and the revered firemen, who had their own section. There are also many deaths from stagecoach accidents, mining cave-ins, suicides, and train accidents.

Some of the more notable burials include:

Mary Jane Simpson, a mule who died in the fire of 1875.

Harriett James, who died July 1875; she killed herself with strychnine because her husband wouldn't stop wrestling.

Mrs. Henry Dods drank strychnine while fighting with her husband over parenting, She fixed him dinner before killing herself.

James McKay, while arguing over religion with his wife, went into his cellar and cut his own throat.

Fred Boegle drank strychnine over unrequited love.

Comstock Cemetery Foundation

Next, you can visit the historic churches in town. The ***St. Paul's Episcopal Church*** burned down along with many other buildings in the fire of 1875. Virginia City's wealth made it possible to rebuild in a year.

Across the street is ***St. Mary's in the Mountains Catholic Church***. The original St. Mary's was built in 1860, and when the Civil War ended in 1865, the St. Mary's bell was rung. The current St. Mary's was built in 1868. There is also a ***Presbyterian Church*** in Virginia City, built in the 1860s.

Don't miss the *Slammer Museum and Jail* within the *Storey County Courthouse* building. It was built in 1876 and is the star of the show, with its ornate decorative façade.

The museum contains some interesting artifacts including original bunkbeds and artwork on the walls, along with a lovely ball and chain ensemble.

Pay a visit to the famous *Fourth Ward School*, built in 1875, with an authentic classroom just as it was in 1936 when the last class graduated.

Virginia City is full of saloons. Among the more notable ones is the famous ***Bucket of Blood Saloon***, built in 1876, after the great fire of 1875.

Another special drinking spot is the ***Red Dog***. It's the venue where the Grateful Dead, and Janis Joplin's Big Brother and the Holding Company began their careers.

As you walk around Virginia City, you might be lucky enough to encounter some four-legged buddies too.

For a change of pace, pay a visit to the ***Comstock Fire Museum***, a donations-only museum. It's in a firehouse built in 1864 and contains fire wagons from the 1840s.

Other buildings you shouldn't miss are the ***Piper's Opera House***, built in 1885, the ***Graves Mansion***, built in 1868, the ***Comstock Mill, The Way it Was*** Museum, and the ***Mark Twain Museum.*** Varney

In Virginia City, you can take a ***trolley tour***, or you can take an ***antique train***. I chose the train option, so I climbed aboard a train powered by a 1916 steam engine, and the car I was sitting in was built in the 1920s. It's a great way to see this special place.

How to get to Virginia City:

Virginia City is 26 miles south-east of Reno, off of I-580 and Hwy 341.

Ghost story:

In Virginia City, at the *Delta Saloon*, there is a faro table, known as the *"Suicide Table"* Many have lost money playing Faro here, and are said to haunt the saloon. "Black Jake" who owned the faro table originally lost $70,000 in one night and promptly killed himself. In 1890, the new owner of the table lost $86,000 and also killed himself. Their ghosts, and many others, are said to haunt the Delta Saloon.

The **Washoe Club** is another favorite haunting site. In fact, it was the subject of an episode of a popular paranormal television show. The building dates from the 1860s and was a hang-out for new millionaires.

There is a **crypt** in the building where bodies were kept until the ground thawed out from winter, so graves could be dug. At least two ghosts have been seen, the "Lady in Blue" and a little girl. Oberding

Profiles in history:

Two brothers, **Hosea,** and **Ethan Allen Grosh** came up from California to look for gold near what is now Virginia City. They noticed a blue-tinted ore that other miners were throwing away. They took a sample of the ore and analyzed it, finding silver. They kept the find to themselves, writing only to their father.

On a hot August morning in 1858, Hosea had an accident, driving a sharp pickaxe into his foot. His foot became infected, and Hosea Grosh died on Sept. 7, 1858. Ethan Allen worked the claim alone, missing his dead brother desperately.

He left with his ore samples on a trip to California to winter there. Leaving in late October, Ethan Allen and his companion R. M. Bucke became trapped by snow and suffered severe frostbite. At the end of the journey Bucke had one of his legs amputated, but Ethan Allan wanted to keep his legs. Ethan Allan died of his injury Dec 19, 1858, three months after his brother. [Oberding]

Henry Comstock, for whom the Comstock Lode is named, found out about the deaths of the two brothers, and took over the claim, confiscating all of the Grosh' brothers' equipment. This was the site of the Ophir Mine, bringing silver wealth to Virginia City.

Henry Comstock foolishly sold the claim for a mere $10,000. Comstock left Nevada and lived in Montana, broke and without friends. In 1870, he committed suicide by shooting himself. He is buried in Bozeman, Montana. [Oberding]

—◦❖◦—

Voices from the past:

"frame shanties, pitched together as if by accident; tents of canvas, of blankets, of brush, of potato sacks and old shirts with empty whiskey barrels for chimneys, smoky hovels of wood and stone; coyote holes in the mountain side forcibly seized and held by men; pits and shafts with smoke issuing from every crevice." **West J. Ross, visiting Virginia City in 1860.**

*"Went with Dr. Hiller, assisted by Dr. Pilking & amputate the leg of Robert Cline, whose right leg was so badly crushed above the ankle by a quartz wagon...took it off about 6 inches above the knee – mortifaction extends still farther up, & he will die..."***Alfred Doten Journal, November 15, 1866, Virginia City.**

Carson City

*C*arson City was settled by John Fremont in the 1840s and
named for Kit Carson, the mountain man in his expedition.
In the historic district of Carson City you need to walk the Kit Car-

son Trail, a historic stroll past many stately and beautiful homes. As you walk along, be sure to see the ***Governor's Mansion*** built in 1908.

Another notable and beautiful home is the ***Bliss Mansion***, which was built in 1879. It's the first home in Nevada piped for natural gas lighting. Carson City, Nevada

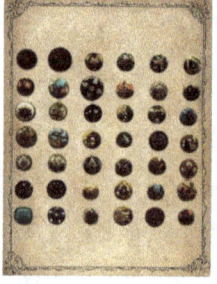

Also in Carson City is the wonderful ***Nevada State Museum***, a nice assortment of history. I started to pass quickly by the button exhibit until I looked closely at the display of spectacular buttons from all over the world.

Each button is a miniature work of art in glass and enamel. The shoe buttons were especially fascinating. Nevada State Museum

One of the artifacts in the museum is the collection of dental equipment from the first lady dentist in Nevada along with some of her favorite extracted teeth. She called it her "unruly" tooth collection. Nevada State Museum

Don't miss the fossilized bones of an ancient horse and a mammoth, both found in Nevada. The museum also features a huge WWI exhibit and weapons hall, with a crossbow from the 1400s. It's a very eclectic museum, well presented.

How to get to Carson City:

Carson City is the capitol of Nevada, and is located about 32 miles south of Reno, off of I-580.

Profiles in history:

Dr. Helen Shipley was born in Reno, Nevada in 1870. She graduated from the University of California's College of Dentistry in San Francisco in 1897, with a degree in dental surgery. She practiced dentistry in Goldfield, from 1906 to 1912, and in Tonopah, from 1912 to 1926. She practiced in Reno her last twenty years as a dentist, and retired in 1946.

Genoa

*G*enoa is a beautiful town, and the oldest settlement in Nevada. It dates from 1851. Genoa has shady streets, a lovely park, and the *Mormon Station*.

The original building burned down and was replaced by the current building in the 1940's.

The artifacts are all original, and include wagons, a sharpening stone, grist mill, and countless artifacts inside the house.

Don't miss the set of homemade skis and a homemade crib belonging to Snowshoe Thompson.

Mormon Station, Genoa, Nevada

How to get to Genoa:

Genoa is located about 12 miles southwest of Carson City on Hwy 395.

Ghost story:

When I visited Mormon Station, I spoke with a medium who works for the Park Service at the station. She had a recording of spirit voices, which she played back for me, including a young pony express rider. She asked him how he liked what he was doing, and he answered, "work and sleep."

Another spirit voice was that of "Snowshoe Thompson" a Norwegian, who delivered mail on skis when the Pony Express couldn't get through the snow-covered Sierras. She asked him about the little crib he made for his son, and he answered, "my little Viking."

Profiles in history:

John "Snowshoe" Thompson was born in Norway in 1827 and came to the United States in 1837 with his mother. He is famous for carrying the mail by skiing over the Sierra Nevada Mountains during the winter, on skis he made himself.

He skied from Placerville to Carson City, a distance of about 100 miles in 3 days, and returned in just two days. Sometimes the pack of mail could weigh as much as 100 pounds, and the snow was often 30 to 50 feet deep. Thompson delivered mail from 1856 to 1876, and yet he was never paid for his services.

He died of appendicitis and pneumonia on May 15, 1876 and is buried in Genoa, Nevada. His little boy, Arthur Thomas, died of diphtheria two years after him and is buried next to his father.

Fort Churchill

*F*ort Churchill was built in 1860 and named after Sylvester Churchill, Inspector General of the US Army.

The fort's purpose was to guard the pony express run. Hundreds of soldiers were stationed there, to guard against Indian attacks. The fort is in ruins, but the grounds are spectacular.

I loved the desolate look of the *hospital*, and I can't imagine what it must have been like to get sick in this place. At the fort hospital, they were allowed one hospital matron for every twenty patients.

In addition to the hospital duties, the doctor was also responsible for sanitation duties at the fort, including disposing of the garbage. Nevada State Parks

Fort Churchill was abandoned nine years later in 1869, and the soldiers remains were removed in 1884 to Carson City.

The only remains left in the *cemetery* are those of the Buckland family, Samuel, his wife Eliza, and five of their eight children. They were pioneers who helped to feed the soldiers at the fort.

As you stroll around Fort Churchill, don't miss the weaponry in its own little enclosure outside.

The **Visitor's Center** has a nice collection of artifacts including a Pony Express Bible, and tools of fort life.

Buckland Station, across from Fort Churchill, was a stagecoach stop, and family home of the Bucklands, who are still buried at Fort Churchill. It's a beautiful home, but not open to visit.

The house was built by Samuel Buckland, an early pioneer who arrived in 1859. He sold supplies and food to Fort Churchill, pony express riders, and travelers of the Overland Stage Company. Corbett

How to get to Fort Churchill and Buckland Station:

Fort Churchill is located off of US Route 95 Alternate, 8 miles south of Hwy 50, near the town of Silver Springs. Buckland Station is a bit further down Fort Churchill Road.

A moment in time:

Three brothers named Williams started up a station 10 miles east of Buckland station. Only one brother, James O. Williams, lived to tell the tale of the massacre that happened there in early May of 1860.

James had been out of town, and when he reached the station, he found his two brothers, 22 year-old Daniel, and 33 year-old Oscar, lying dead on the ground. There were others including 25 year-old Samuel Sullivan from New York, and 25 year-old James Fleming, also from New York. One additional man, Dutch Phil lay dead too.

The men appeared to have been mutilated, tortured, and possibly burned alive, which was a custom of Paiute Indians of the area. Williams station was a charred ruin, and all of the animals were missing.

The **Massacre at Williams Station** resulted in the Pyramid Lake Indian War. Historians believe that the massacre occurred because someone at Williams Station had kidnapped some Indian women and held them prisoner in a cave for several days. The massacre may have been revenge for the kidnappings. [Corbett]

———————

Voices from the past:

"Wanted, young, skinny, wiry fellows not over eighteen. Must be expert riders, willing to risk death daily. Orphans preferred. Wages $25 a week" **job posting from a San Francisco newspaper, March 1860.** [Corbett]

"Greatest of all inventions to me, because it affected me directly, is the telegraph. In the two minutes we used to be allowed to change horses at a station, Western Union now sends a message to New York or even London, The telegraph to-day does in a second what it took eighty young men and hundreds of horses eight days to do when I was a rider in the Pony Express."

William Campbell, pony express rider, at age 94. Corbett

Fun facts about the Pony Express:

- The Pony Express ran from 1860 to 1861 and was replaced by the telegraph.

- The route ran from St. Joseph, Missouri to Sacramento, California, a distance of 1900 miles

- Highway 50, known as the "loneliest road in America" was part of the mail route from Sacramento to Salt Lake City in 1851.

- There were 190 stations along the route, when the Pony Express was in peak operation.

- Each station was equipped with 2 agents, 1 station keeper, and 1 assistant.

- There were 420 horses used at peak times, along with 80 riders.

John Fisher, John Hancock, and Billy Fisher, Pony Express Riders

- Pony Express riders weighed an average of 100 to 120 pounds, and their average age was 19.

- Horses were usually half-wild mustangs, famous for their speed and the fact that they never got tired.

- They rode an average speed of 7 miles per hour, which meant that it took them an average of 10 days to complete the trip.

- Each rider rode 60 to 120 miles before changing riders.

- The fastest ride ever was 7.5 days to deliver Abraham Lincoln's Inaugural address.

- William C. "Buffalo Bill" Cody rode 322 miles in 21 hours and 40 minutes using 21 horses.

- Riders were paid $120 to $125 per month.

- A letter cost $5 in gold, paid in advance.[Corbett]

Fallon

*F*allon has a remarkable museum, called the ***Churchill County Museum***. It was voted the best small town museum in America, and when you enter, you will know why. It has an enormous and eclectic collection of artifacts, antiques and memorabilia. It's a donations-only museum, which is a relic of the past too.

Some of my favorites are a beautiful yellow silk dress from the 1920's, an early bicycle, and a wreath made of human hair.

The museum also houses a generous collection of vehicles including horse-drawn buggies and wagons, early fire engines, an early school bus. and a steam operated road roller.

Churchill County Museum

How to get to Fallon:

Fallon is located about 60 miles east of Reno, off of Hwy. 50.

New Pass Station

N ew Pass Station was built in 1861 and served as an important stop for the Butterfield Stage Line on the route from
Salt Lake City to Genoa, Nevada.

Stagecoaches would stop here for water and supplies before continuing on. Butterfield sold out to Wells Fargo, but the railroad made stage travel obsolete. Wells Fargo Stage shut down in 1869. [Corbett]

I camped here for the night, and was greeted by some spectacular wild horses. They were shy and didn't approach very closely. It was a wonderful experience.

How to get to New Pass Stagecoach Station:

New Pass Station is located 25 miles west of Austin, off of Hwy. 50.

Cold Springs Station

I n Cold Springs, Nevada, you can find the ruins of the *Cold Springs Pony Express Station*, stagecoach stop, and telegraph office. It's hard to imagine the solitude of the place and what life must have been like for these guys.

A station master was killed by Indians in May, 1860, at Cold Springs Station.

Archaeological excavations in the 1970's at Cold Springs uncovered hundreds of glass pieces from wine, whiskey, and beer bottles.

Drinking alcohol was forbidden, but the rule was not enforced, so pony express riders were sometimes seen falling off of their horses, drunk. [Corbett]

How to get to Cold Springs Pony Express Station:

The Cold Springs Pony Express Station is off of Hwy 50, about 59 miles east of the town of Fallon.

Voices from the past:

"The station was a wretched place half built and wholly unroofed; the four boys, an exceedingly rough set, ate standing, and neither paper nor pencil was known amongst them..."

"*The station house was no unfit object in such a scene, roofless and hairless. filthy and squalid, with a smoky fire in one corner and a table in the center of an impure floor, the walls open to every wind and the interior full of dust.*" **Explorer Sir Richard Burton, on Cold Springs and Sand Springs Pony Express Stations, October 1860.**

"*It is a hard life, setting aside the chance of death, no less than three murders have been committed by Indians during this year, the work is severe; the diet is sometimes reduced to wolf mutton, or a little boiled wheat and rye, and the drink to brackish water, a pound of tea comes occasionally, but the droughty souls are always out of whiskey and tobacco.*" **Explorer Sir Richard Burton, on finding Pony Express employees living in a hole in Eastern Nevada, October 1860.** Corbett

A word about Pony Express history:

Before horses were used to carry mail, a mail carrying system known as "**jackass mail**" was tried out. George Chorpenning and Absolom Woodward contracted with the federal government to use mules to haul the mail. Jackass mail was short-lived, and its founders were as well. Woodward was killed by Indians, and Chorpenning died penniless.

Camels were tried out too. Jefferson Davis, secretary of war came up with the idea in 1853. It was a big hit with Bible readers, but the camels didn't like the rocky terrain. Leather boots were made to protect their feet, but the camels were a failure. Some were sold as circus animals, and others were simply let loose in the desert.
Corbett

Grimes Point
Archaeological
Area

The ***Grimes Point Archaeological Area*** is fascinating, with ancient petroglyphs, chiseled into hard rock surfaces. Sadly, some of them have been chiseled out, but there are still a lot to see. These petroglyphs are believed to be between 7000 and 9000 years old. Balfour

How to get to Grimes Point Archaeological Area:

The Grimes Point Archaeological Area is located off of Hwy 50 about 12 miles east of the town of Fallon.

A word about petroglyphs and pictographs:

Petroglyphs were made by taking river rock and heating it and then cooling it suddenly so it cracks to form a sharp tool. This tool was used to chisel along with another stone for a hammer to peck or incise the designs on rock. A thick desert coating called a patina was removed to expose the lighter rock underneath.

A ***petroglyph panel*** is a group of petroglyphs that tell a story. The Hopi describe the purpose of petroglyphs like this:

The Creator told the Hopi to make their mark on the land saying, "We were here." They built homes with rock, painted pottery and broke it into pieces when they left the land, and they put markings on walls so they could remember an area during migration. Indigenous people view petroglyphs as history, part of their culture, a culture that is ongoing. ^{Chino}

Pictographs, are painted instead of incised. They are drawn pictures using minerals like hematite mixed with a binder such as animal fat, urine, or oil to make paint. The spiral sun symbol commonly represented may show Hopi migration, where they come from and where they have been. The images talk to the current Hopi people about their past history.

Pictograph colors are:

- Black, which is made with yellow ochre, pinon gum, and sumac

- Red, which is made with red ochre and mahogany root

- Yellow, which is made with rabbitbrush

- Plant oils and animal fats were used as binders

Central Nevada

Berlin, Nevada

Austin

A ustin began its life in 1862, when a man went searching for a missing horse. He found silver instead. Austin was named for Austin, Texas and grew to a population of around 7000 people.

In 1863, Austin became the seat of Lander County. At its height, Austin contained hotels, banks, and streets lit by gaslights. Varney

As you walk along the streets of Austin, you can visit the *Gridley Store*, built in 1863, *St. George's Episcopal Church*, built in 1878, The *Leland House*, built in the 1860s, and the *International Hotel,* which was moved to Austin from Virginia City in 1863. You can also pay a visit to the local haunt, the *Lander County Courthouse* and the *Austin cemetery*.

How to get to Austin:

Austin is located in central Nevada, off of Hwy 50.

Ghost story:

The Lander County Courthouse is said to be haunted by the ghost of **Rufus Anderson**, who was hung on October 30, 1868 for shooting and killing a man. The first attempt to hang Rufus failed when the knot broke. A second attempt also failed.

At this point, spectators wanted the execution to be stopped, but guards stepped in to make sure justice was done. On the third attempt, Rufus finally met his maker. People visiting the courthouse have heard the noisy sounds of footsteps going up and down the stairs, and doors opening and closing. Oberding

A word about hanging:

Before an inmate was hung, the inmate was weighed. A sandbag was filled to about the same weight as the inmate. Then, the sandbag was used in an experiment to find out the correct length of rope. The goal was for the inmate to die quickly. If the rope was too long, the inmate could be decapitated. If the rope was too short, the inmate would slowly strangle to death.

If the rope length was "just right" the inmate would die quickly, with a broken neck. Once the right length of rope was found, the execution was ready. The inmate was led up the stairs of the scaffold, blindfolded, with arms and legs tied. The noose was placed around the neck, a trapdoor was sprung, and the inmate fell through the opening to a quick death.

Profiles in history:

Ruel C. Gridley, a resident of Austin, built the Gridley Store out of stone back in 1863. Gridley is famous for losing a bet on an election. As a consequence of making a bad wager, he had to carry a 50 pound sack of flour through town.

At the end of his "journey" he auctioned off the flour sack, with the proceeds going to the U.S. Sanitary Commission, a charity organization formed to help wounded Union soldiers.

The residents of Austin bought, and then re-auctioned, and rebought the sack until the day's total reached $6000. Gridley ended up with the sack in the end. He finally sold the sack in 1865 in St. Louis, raising $275,000 for the charity. That charity is now the Red Cross. Gridley lapsed into poverty and died six years later. Town of Austin

Berlin

B *erlin* started out late in the mining boom, in 1895 when silver mining began. By 1908, Berlin had a population of between 200 and 300 people.

The town had a post office, an assay office, a union hall, stage station, and miners' shacks. Berlin is in a gorgeous location. It's very remote, which only adds to the desolate feeling. It's a true ghost town.

As you walk around Berlin, you can visit about a dozen historic buildings including a *machine shop, stage station, assay office, the Berlin mill,* and the *cemetery*.

You can also visit the *adobe house*, built in the late 1800s. It was owned by Henry Joseph, an early pioneer who worked as a freighter, carrying loads to and from Tonopah.

Berlin Ichthyosaur Park is next to the town of Berlin, and it's the home of the largest ichthyosaurs ever found. There are nine skeletons jumbled up in this quarry. The largest skeleton the experts believe to be 70 feet long, with a skull 10 feet long. Ichthyosaurs gave birth to live young which were 6 feet long at birth. These ichthyosaurs swam in the water that is now Central Nevada 225 million years ago.

Varney

How to get to Berlin and the Ichthyosaur Park:

Berlin is located 290 miles north of Las Vegas, off of Hwy 95 north. The park is next to the ghost town.

Belmont

B*elmont* began when silver was discovered near there in 1865. Belmont's most notable building is the two-story brick *courthouse*, a much-photographed historic building. Charles

Manson even carved his name into a first-floor doorframe. He camped in the Monitor Valley close to Belmont, in 1969. [Varney]

By 1866, Belmont contained stores, restaurants, saloons, a drug store, a brewery, a bank, the Austin & Belmont Stage Company, and a dentist's office.

As you walk around Belmont, you can see the ruins of several historic buildings, including the *First National Bank, Cosmopolitan Saloon, a mercantile, market,* and *hardware store.*

Also pay a visit to the *Belmont Cemetery*, one of the prettiest cemeteries I've ever seen.

How to get to Belmont:

Belmont is in central Nevada, 265 miles north of Las Vegas, off of Hwy 95 north.

Tonopah

*T*onopah is an old mining town that has a wonderful hotel known as the *Mizpah*.

It was built in 1907 and is filled with antique Victorian furnishings that look like they just came off of the Titanic.

There is a nice little *mining museum* and *mining shacks* you can visit.

How to get to Tonopah:

Tonopah is about 211 miles North of Las Vegas off of Hwy 95.

Ghost story:

The Mizpah Hotel has a ghost named the ***"Lady in Red.*** " She is said to have been murdered there on the 5th floor. I didn't see her while I was there. I think my ferocious sheltie, Sadie, probably scared her away.

The Lady in Red was a prostitute who conducted her business with Mizpah patrons in the 1920s. A wealthy man is said to have killed her in a room on the fifth floor in a fit of rage after learning he was only one of her many customers.

Legend has it that the ghost of the lady roams the hotel to this day.

Another version of the tale says her husband caught the woman cheating on him at the hotel after he had missed a train. He then beat her to death in a room, now often requested by guests who believe in the paranormal.

Rhyolite

*R**hyolite,** founded in 1904, was named for the volcanic rock found in the area. It became populated when a large strike of gold was found, as part of the Bullfrog Mining District.

By 1908, Rhyolite had an estimated population of between 4000 and 8000 people. The town also boasted running water, telephones, and electricity. Rhyolite contained a stock exchange, board of trade, hospital, miners' union, ice plant, hotels, and stores.

For leisure time, Rhyolite had an opera house, ice cream parlor, and public swimming pools. The town was also served by three railroads. Varney

As you walk around Rhyolite, check out the ***Tom T. Kelly Bottle House*** built in 1906. The house is made out of 30,000 Adolphus Busch beer bottles.

My favorite structure is a compact little building known as the *brothel*, built in 1907.

Other buildings you can see include the *jail* built in 1907, the *railroad depot* built in 1909, the *John S. Cook Bank* built in 1908, the *Porter Brothers Store* built in 1906, and the 1909 *schoolhouse*, which is in ruins.

You can also visit the *Bullfrog-Rhyolite Cemetery* nearby.

How to get to Rhyolite:

Rhyolite, Nevada is about 4 miles west of Beatty, which is 116 miles north of Las Vegas, off of Hwy 95 north.

My story:

I have fond memories of dropping my cell phone through the iron bars of the brothel and into the building while trying to take a photo. Fortunately, I retrieved it with a long stick, but it took a bit of work.

Eastern Nevada

Ward Charcoal Ovens

Ward Charcoal Ovens

The **Ward Charcoal Ovens** are magnificent, with stonework that looks more like a medieval castle than an oven.

They get their name from the nearby town of Ward, which is no longer standing. The ovens remain, a unique testament to the skill of stonemasons.

These were built in 1876 and used through 1879. They processed silver ore during the mining days. Later, the ovens became shelter for travelers and a hideout for stagecoach robbers.

How to get to Ward Charcoal Ovens:

From Ely, Nevada, take Hwy. 50 south for 13 miles to the Ward Charcoal Ovens State Park turnoff. Travel about 5 miles to Cave Valley Road which leads to the ovens.

Pioche

P*ioche* is a picturesque little town, founded in the 1870s. It has a very interesting ***"Boot Hill" Cemetery*** with a "***Murderer's Row"*** that is separated from the rest of the cemetery.

In the 1870s, 72 people were killed before anyone died of natural causes. My favorite is a tombstone which reads "killed over a dispute about a dog"

The *Pioche Tramway*, from the 1920s, delivered ore from the mine to the mill using gravity and a 5 horsepower motor. Delivery in 1928 cost 6 cents per ton of ore.

As you walk around town, visit the *Thompson's Opera House*, built in 1873, and the *Mountain View Hotel* built in 1895. You can also see an old miner's cabin with furnishings.

The ***town museum*** is in the brick courthouse, which also contains the ***jail***. Pioche is a nice place to spend a few hours.

How to get to Pioche:

Pioche, Nevada is 186 miles northeast of Las Vegas, off of Hwy 93 north.

Southern Nevada

Las Vegas Bay

Gold Point

G *old Point* started out with several names. When lime was found in 1868, the town was called Lime Point. When silver was found in the 1880s, the town was known as Hornsilver. The town had over 200 buildings including stores, saloons, and a post office. In 1927, gold was discovered in the hills, and the town became Gold Point. ^{Varney}

As you walk around Gold Point, you can visit ***Mitchell's Mercantile, Expiration Mercantile, Turf Saloon***, and ***Gold Dust Saloon***, all built in 1908. There are also many miner's residences still standing in Gold Point.

How to get to Gold Point:

Gold Point is off of Hwy 95, about 165 miles north of Las Vegas. Turn left onto route 266, go 7.5 miles, and turn left again on route 774. Go 8 more miles into town.

A word about mining terms and superstitions:

Some common terms thrown about in the world of mining include:

Prospecting-looking for material to be mined, usually in the form of a gold or silver vein trapped within quartz. This is known as "blossom rock."

Placer mining-to find superficial deposits of gold in streams and rivers

Lode mining-to find deposits of precious metals enclosed in rock

Miners worked in extremely hazardous conditions, and the danger of their jobs may have led them to become highly superstitious. These are just a few of the superstitions miners believed in:

- Women were bad luck in the mines, especially if the woman was a redhead. It meant someone would die.

- Someone would also die if a black cat or a dog entered the mine.

- Whistling in a mine drove away good spirits and invited bad ones. Whistling was also believed to cause vibrations in the earth, prompting a cave-in.

- A cave-in was most likely to happen between midnight and 4 AM.

- Miners would often quit a day early because they believed they would be injured or killed on their last shift.

Goldfield

*G*oldfield was born in 1902 when two prospectors where shown gold samples by a Shoshone Indian prospector. The two men originally named the site Grandpa, because they wanted it to be the granddaddy of all gold fields. ^{Varney}

In 1903, the town was renamed Goldfield, because it was a way to attract people to the town. People flocked to Goldfield, and by the late summer of 1904, ten thousand dollars in gold per day was being pulled out of the hills. During the 15 years of mining, Goldfield produced more than 80 million dollars in gold.

Goldfield eventually held 20,000 people, had four railroads, brick buildings, electricity, running water, four schools, and two stock exchanges.

The **_Goldfield Hotel_** was built in 1908. It cost $500,000 to build, had 154 rooms, and guests enjoyed fine dining featuring lobster. Goldfield was damaged by a monsoon in 1913, and a huge fire in 1923.

As you walk around the streets of Goldfield, look out for other notable buildings, including the *Nixon-Wingfield Block*, and the *Goldfield High School,* both built in 1907. You can also see the *Esmeralda County Courthouse*, built in 1908, the *firehouse museum*, and the picturesque *cemetery.*

How to get to Goldfield:

Goldfield is located 180 miles north of Las Vegas on Hwy 95.

Ghost story:

The Goldfield Hotel is said to be haunted by a few ghosts. The most famous are a pair of ghosts, *George Wingfield*, who was part owner of the hotel and one of Nevada's wealthiest men at the time, and *Elizabeth*, a young prostitute, who was in love with Wingfield.

Elizabeth became pregnant and Wingfield forced her to remain in seclusion in the hotel. She was chained to a radiator in room 109. She gave birth, and she died in the hotel, either by starvation or murder by George Wingfield. He then threw the newborn down a mineshaft under the hotel. Visitors have stated they smell Wingfield's cigar smoke and sense his malev-

olent presence. They also sense the sad presence of Elizabeth haunting room 109. [Oberding]

Valley of Fire

T he ***Valley of Fire*** is a spectacular canyon located near the
town of Overton, Nevada. It's a joy to walk through the
canyon of red sandstone and to see the petroglyphs left behind

by the Ancestral Puebloan people who lived here from 300 BC to 1150 AD. [Finch]

The dark patina on the rocks left by nature provided an excellent background for the images carved by the ancient artists.

Typical subjects were humanoid figures, game animals including bighorn sheep and antelope, and geometric figures.

How to get to the Valley of Fire:

The Valley of Fire is located at 29450 Valley of Fire Hwy.

Las Vegas

T he sparkling city of **Las Vegas** beckons people from all over the world to gamble, enjoy a show, shop, and absorb the glitz.

To truly absorb Las Vegas, you need to see Old Vegas. Take a walk down *Fremont Street,* see the amazing light show, and enjoy one of the best places to people watch in the world.

There is a lot more to Las Vegas, including some interesting history. To find the history, you need to first exit the casino.

Visit the *Old Mormon Fort* to find out where Las Vegas began. It was the first non-native building in the Las Vegas valley, built in 1855.

30 Mormon settlers came into the Las Vegas Valley, bringing their belongings in sturdy wagons, a couple of which greet you as you enter the fort.

It's an amazing step back into history, and well worth the $3 entrance fee.

There are many artifacts inside the house within the fort, including the first flag flown over Vegas, a loom, and furnishings.

As you walk the grounds, you will see old wagons, and a vine-covered enclosure called the *Bowery*. It's where the first settlers held meetings. Old Mormon Fort

Another very worthwhile stop is the *Clark County Museum* on the outskirts of Vegas.

It's a neat little indoor-outdoor museum with buildings, vehicles, and artifacts taken from different areas of Nevada, spanning the State's history.

First, enjoy the outside, as you walk down a serene, tree-lined street containing houses from different time periods.

It's an amazing assortment of houses, each furnished with items from the time. It's a bit interesting seeing items you grew up with, now being called antiques.

In a different outdoor section of the museum, you can see old miner's shacks, a toll house, and some fascinating old vehicles aging gracefully in the sun.

Inside the museum, you can find early gambling machines, each one an ornate work of art.

There are old slot machines, and an early Wheel-of-Fortune, my personal favorite. Clark County Mus.

The *Tule Springs Fossil Beds National Monument,* just on the edge of North Vegas is a new national monument, and as of my visit, there were no facilities or visitors center, just acres of canyons to walk through.

In 1933, mammoth remains were found here. In 1962, major excavations unearthed the bones of mammoths, camels, bison, ground sloths, and North American lions.

The fossils date from 3,000 to 200,000 years ago. Much of the area is still unexcavated. Tule Springs Fossil Beds

How to get to Las Vegas historic sites:

The Old Mormon Fort is located at 500 E Washington Ave.

The Clark County Museum is located at 1830 S Boulder Hwy.

The Tule Springs Fossil Beds is located at North Aliante Pkwy and Hwy 95 north.

Ash Meadows Wildlife Refuge

The *Ash Meadows National Wildlife Refuge* is a beautiful way to spend a few hours. The wooden walkways meander through grasses, trees, and around deep pools of crystal clear water.

The refuge was named for the numerous ash trees first described by explorers in 1893.

There is a historically significant structure here too, named the *Longstreet Cabin*. The stone cabin was built by Jack Longstreet, a famous gunman of early Nevada.

The Longstreet Cabin is built over a spring, keeping it much cooler in the summer than the surrounding area. Longstreet and his second wife lived in the cabin from 1895 to 1899. Ash Meadows

How to get to Ash Meadows Wildlife Refuge:

Ash Meadows Wildlife Refuge is located 90 miles Northwest of Las Vegas off of Hwy. 95.

Profiles in history:

Jack Longstreet first becomes known to history in 1880, when he was a prospector in Arizona. He became a saloon owner in 1890, where he kidnapped the town mining foreman, forcing him to pay the Paiute workers with regular paychecks, instead of worthless scrip.

He spoke the Paiute language and had several Native American wives. Longstreet homesteaded in Ash Meadows from 1889 to 1907. He built his famous cabin at Ash Meadows when he was in his '50s, and later sold it for $30,000. Longstreet stashed his money, steering clear of the bank failures which happened in 1907. He died in 1928. Ash Meadows

Death Valley
National Park

*D*eath Valley is a remarkable national park. It's the largest national park in the continental United States, and it is the hottest, driest, and lowest in elevation. At its lowest point, Death Valley is 282 feet below sea level.

Native Americans lived in Death Valley beginning in 7000 BC, and up until 1000 AD. The first non-Native Americans were a group of prospectors making their way to the California Gold Rush in 1849. This group named the area Death Valley because one of the group died there.

As you drive through Death Valley, you can see what's left of the 1914 *Ashford Mill*. The mill was owned by the Ashford brothers, who processed gold ore here from the Golden Treasure Mine.

How to get to Death Valley National Park:

One entrance to Death Valley National Park is on hwy. SR 374, about 54 miles from the town of Beatty, Nevada.

Goodsprings

***G**oodsprings* is a cool little town, and a favorite of bikers. It started out in the 1860s as a mining town.

As you walk around town, you can see many old miner's shacks, but the star of Goodsprings is the **Pioneer Saloon,** built in 1913.

In 1942, It was here that Clark Gable waited for news of whether Carole Lombard survived the plane crash in the nearby mountains. Sadly she did not. Town of Goodsprings, Nevada

How to get to Goodsprings:
Goodsprings is 33 miles south of Las Vegas, off of I-15 south, and Hwy 161 west.

Ghost story:

The Pioneer Saloon in Goodsprings is said to be haunted by a cheating card player named ***Paul Coski.*** He was shot and killed while sitting at a poker table. You can see bullet holes in the ceiling which are thought to be from the shooting.

Some have seen the ghosts of ***Carole Lombard*** and ***Clark Gable*** in the saloon. It was here in 1942 that Gable got the news Lombard had been killed in an airplane crash. There is a spot at the bar where Gable's cigarettes burned the wood where he was sitting, waiting for news. Oberding

Nelson

*N**elson*** is a cool little place, with lots of items both large and small, rusting in the sun.

The area was first explored by the Spanish in 1775 and called "Eldorado" and then mined to death starting in 1859.

Gold and silver were the main minerals. In the early days of Nelson, there were a lot of Civil War deserters and they got into arguments and killed each other on a daily basis. Town of Nelson, Nevada

How to get to Nelson:

Nelson is about 40 miles south of Las Vegas, located off of Hwy 95 south.

Favorite Places to Camp

Las Vegas Bay Campground

Lake Mead Recreational Area has several campgrounds including **Boulder Beach Campground** and **Las Vegas**

Bay Campground, both with spectacular views. Campsites are $20/night, and there are water spigots and toilets, but no showers.

Fort Churchill Campground is right next to Fort Churchill. The campground is nestled in a large grove of trees, providing wonderful shade for comfortable camping. The campground has 20 sites which range $15 to $20 per night. It's a beautiful spot, right next to the Carson River.

Willow Creek Campground

Willow Creek Campground is the perfect home base to explore Ward Charcoal Ovens. The campground is small, and sublimely beautiful, with breathtaking vistas of snow-capped mountains. There are water spigots and toilets but no showers.

Berlin Ichthyosaur Campground is next to Berlin and the Ichthyosaur exhibit. There are 14 spots in this beautiful campground with fire rings, barbeque grills, and covered picnic tables.

Random Thoughts

What History Means to Me

F irst, let me start by sharing with you my opinion of what history isn't. History is not a collection of random dates, names, and places for you to memorize. History is not a dry and uninteresting class you have to pass to graduate.

I believe history is a tangible thing. You can actually *feel* history in the places you go, and the sights you see. I remember walking up to the Acropolis in Athens. I looked down at the well-worn marble steps and wondered about how many ancient philosophers had climbed these very steps, thousands of years ago.

You don't have to go far away to experience the *feeling* of history. If you are lucky enough to live in an old house, you may experience history in your own surroundings. You might say to yourself, *"If only these walls could talk."*

During my travels across the United States, I *felt* history in many, many places. If you travel across the country like I did, you will *feel* the wonderful history of our beautiful country for yourself, and you will never be the same. You will discover what it means to be an American.

Why I did it and why you can too:

I decided to travel across the country by car because I wanted to rediscover America. When I first set out to explore the history of our country, I wanted to find out why America is the greatest country on earth, and what it means to be an American.

The politics of these United States was frightening at the time. Our country was polarized, almost beyond repair. Whether it was Democrats or Republicans, Conservatives, or Liberals, everyone was fighting.

I wanted to rediscover the joy of being an American. I wanted to rediscover our rich history, our unique and wonderful people, our tapestry of multicultural heritage, and our rich natural resources. I thought a road trip by car across eleven western states was a good place to start.

I have a degree in Archaeology, and a passion for all things archaeological. I love history, with a side love of paleontology. It is these three passions that I set my trip agenda around. I set out to discover the archaeological sites, history, and paleontological world of our country.

As I travel and write my books, I get asked all the time, especially by women, "What is it like to travel by yourself? Aren't you scared?" The truth is, I believe everyone should do what I did. It's a wonderful way to discover our country, and to rediscover yourself. The truth is, I'm scared not to travel. Traveling allows you to get to know yourself, in ways not possible when sitting on the couch watching TV.

We tend to spend a lot of our lives tuning out the world and our place within it. When you travel, you are quite literally forced to deal with your own thoughts, emotions, and feelings. You can discover yourself while traveling. You can come to understand what makes you who you are, and how you can perhaps become a better person. Above all, traveling gives you mental clarity to figure out how to live with intent. It's a way to guide your life, not just wait for things to happen.

Travel Tips & Stuff

What You Need to Know

How to get started:

Planning your trip should be one of the most exciting things about it. You want to be spontaneous, but it is also very wise to plan your route, so you can take full advantage of all the time and miles you will invest.

- First, decide your passions. If you love airplanes, trains, or old vehicles, plan your trip around that. If you love gardens or architecture, seek that out as the focus of your trip.

- Next, read and research areas of the country that will let you enjoy what you are interested in.

- Make a list by state and city or town, of what you want to see.

- Take your handy road atlas and locate the areas on the pages.

- Make a tentative route plan, so you have an idea of where you are going.

Travel tip: Avoid trying to plan your trip down to a schedule of days, hours, or minutes. On a road trip, it will be virtually impossible to know where you will be on any given day. If you adhere to a schedule, you are more likely to stress out, and less likely to actually enjoy yourself, which is the whole point.

What you need:

You need to bring along a sense of adventure and a curious mind. You need to ditch the idea of always being on a schedule, and live a little more spontaneously to thoroughly enjoy yourself. Things will happen as you travel, both good things and bad things, and you need to prepare your mind and your soul for day-to-day changes.

So much of our lives are planned out. Between growing up, going to school, finding a career, marriage, kids, or whatever, people have lost much of the ability to be spontaneous. But you must take spontaneity on the trip with you, because you may make detours along the way to see something really spectacular.

So, for the practical stuff you need:

*A great vehicle-*I have a Honda CRV which is fabulous. It's old, a 2004, fully paid for, and will go anywhere. I see humongous RVs on the road, towing a car behind, and all I can think of is, they can't go just anywhere. They are too big. Bad gas mileage, cumbersome to drive, slow, and not agile like my CRV. So, I encourage you, if you want to go car camping and be able to go on remote dirt roads, get an agile vehicle, and Hondas are great.

Travel tip: Don't be afraid to do some modifications to your vehicle. I took one of my back seats out. (after watching a YouTube video) I threw in a twin mattress, a bit of drapery, and some netting. I also put some of those little portable light switches on the inside. I jettisoned anything I hadn't used up to that point. Don't be afraid to get rid of unnecessary stuff.

An awesome camera that you know inside and out. I use a Nikon and it takes wonderful pictures. Don't skimp on a camera, and don't think a cellphone camera is all you need, because you want the best for your beautiful photos.

A hot plate warmer-this little item was indispensable. You need a converter for it so you can plug it in to the cigarette lighter. Place your food inside it, carton and all, and then plug it in. 30 minutes for thawed food, about an hour and a half for frozen food. Boom! You have a hot meal by the time you stop for the night!

Window shades-the best ones are magnetic so you just place them against your windows and they cling to them, obscuring the view inside your car.

━·⊜✦⊜·━

Portable cooler with wheels-another indispensable item that works great and is easy to move around. I use those nifty blue frozen blocks in mine.

━·⊜✦⊜·━

Portable air compressor-this little gem plugs into your cigarette lighter and will inflate your tires if you have a flat. Fortunately, I haven't had to use this yet.

Portable battery charger and power bank-mine comes with battery cables and the power bank, yet once inside the case, it is small enough to put in your glove compartment. This little item, unfortunately, I have had to use, and it saved me.

Portable generator-mine came with a small solar panel, so it can be charged with solar or electricity. It has a decent battery life and also doubles as a light for night-time.

All season clothing-you never know what different states will bring for weather, so take hot weather and cold weather clothes, and a fair amount of shoes appropriate for hiking, or walking, sandals, and slippers, which are nice at night. Also take along a pair of cheap rubber flip-flops to wear in the public showers you might go into.

Your own pillows-I like my own pillows, so I don't wake up with neck cramps, especially after sleeping in the car.

Sleeping bag and cozy blankets-you want to stay warm and layering is everything.

Warm hat, warm socks, and fuzzy jammies to keep you warm for cold nights sleeping in the car.

A great road atlas, and great guidebooks-get one that's easy to read, with great pictures. For a road atlas, just get one that is easy to read.

A word about photography:

Along with a great camera, you need to have a great eye. This is easier than it sounds once you have worked with your camera and are comfortable taking pictures with it. I am not a professional photographer, but I like my pictures and other people do too.

These are my tips for taking great pictures:

- Experiment with taking both horizontal and vertical shots.

- Don't always put the subject of the photo in the middle of the photograph.

- This one is important: pay attention to the foreground, and if possible, have something, a plant or whatever, in the foreground to help give the photo dimension and depth.

- This one is important too: turn around often to see the view you just came from. I do this quite often and some of my best pictures have resulted from when I turned around and took the shot.

You can also take a mental photo. Place an image in your mind that you can call upon later. Use all of your senses to see, hear, smell, and maybe even to taste, what is around you. You have the means to fully experience your surroundings, and that is very important to a traveler. When you take a mental photo, be sure to jot down quick little details about what you saw, heard, smelled, or tasted, so you can jog your memory later.

And last, but not least...don't be posing in front of everything, everywhere, to show that you actually went somewhere. Most people want to see themselves in your photo and be mentally transported there, but they can't if you are there already.

To camp or not to camp:

Car camping is great. I prefer it to sleeping on the cold, hard ground in a tent. I can lock the doors, put my window shades up and be cozy for the night.

That being said, for me there were some do's and don'ts about camp sites. Some people camp in a Walmart parking lot and feel safe. I do not. I believe that if you are in a busy area, you're more likely to be confronted by a nut job who may bother you. Nothing against Walmart.

Same goes for casino parking lots. Many people believe that if they are in a public place, there is less chance of someone bothering them. I don't share this belief. I believe you are safer parked out in the middle of nowhere in the dark. That same nut job who can find you in a parking lot is not about to go driving around on dirt roads to see if anyone is parked there. At least that's my belief. You may not share it, and that's fine. Park and camp wherever you feel safe.

I don't go for rest areas either because they have a track record of incidents happening to people in rest areas, especially women travelers.

So, where do I camp? In state or national campgrounds, wildlife sanctuaries, or off on a dirt road somewhere, usually out in the middle of nowhere.

There are definitely times when I stay in a motel. I use Hotels.com because I like their stay 10 nights, get 1 night free deal. So, I book a hotel or motel if:

- The weather is too hot or too cold, or too rainy

- I am in a city and plan to stay awhile

- I'm tired of camping, need a shower, or my body hurts

- I need to do laundry

A word about safety:

When you are a woman traveling alone, it's critical to keep a low profile. Don't tell people you are traveling alone, where you are staying, or any other personal information.

I don't go to bars or get drunk. I'm not preaching but you are on your own, in a city or town you've never been to, and you don't know anyone, so it's not the time to lose control of what you are doing. When you are in control, you are better able to decide which people you want to get to know better.

Travel tip: If you feel vulnerable traveling alone, that's OK. Vulnerability is part of passion, and traveling is a passionate thing to do. You can put one of those family stickers on your vehicle to indicate to others that you are not traveling alone, which can help you feel more secure.

Maintain your connections:

When you are traveling alone, there is a definite sense of disconnection. It feels almost like you are the only one in the world, traveling through space and time. That's why it's critical to keep your connections to loved ones active.

Be on Facebook while you are traveling. You may not have internet a lot of the time, or the internet will be poor. Consider paying to have your phone be a hotspot. It's a little bit of money per month, but it's worth it and has saved me from being without internet. I love the convenience of it, and you will too.

Plan your journey around visiting family members or friends you haven't seen for a long time, or people that are good friends. When you see people you know, it will ground you, so you can continue traveling.

Check in by phone with loved ones. They worry about you, and it's good for both of you to stay connected no matter where you are.

Consider traveling with a pet. I started my trip with my beloved 14-year-old sheltie named Sadie. She didn't make it to the end of the trip. I lost her to bladder cancer about four months in. My Sadie was special, and I will never forget my first traveling buddy.

It took me a solid year to decide on getting another dog. I poured over profiles of rescue dogs, looking for a little buddy I could take care of. Best Friends Animal Society in Kanab, Utah, had my perfect match. I now have Rosie, an 8 year-old sheltie that looks just like Sadie and has many of the same mannerisms. Life is good again.

I highly recommend Best Friends Animal Society if you are looking for a pet. They have 3000 acres and house up to 1600 animals at one time including dogs, cats, horses, pigs, and just about everything else. The dedicated people at Best Friends are wonderful both to you, and your potential pet.

Travel tip: One of the easiest and best ways I stay connected while traveling is to offer to take a photo for someone I don't know. Many couples, families, or singles would love to have more pictures of themselves traveling. It's an easy and quick way to have a connection with a fellow traveler, and it's good manners too.

Practical matters:

You need to have an address to send your mail to. Keep in touch with whomever is nice enough to do this for you.

You will also need to come back occasionally to register your car, vote, go to doctor visits, and take care of any other business. You can't leave it all behind, as tempting as that may be.

Bad things that happened:

Remember when I said you need to take spontaneity with you on your trip? Well, there were many times when I used my spontaneity skillset.

The government shutdown happened smack dab in the middle of my travels. That meant that all of the National Monuments were closed. I did a lot of driving and circling around.

I also did a lot of circling around trying to avoid natural disasters. I traveled through Paradise, California shortly before a massive fire happened there. I tried to travel through the area again but was pushed out by massive flooding. My latest event was camping in Canyonville, Oregon and waking up to flames creeping down the hillside. That was day one of the Canyonville fire.

Besides being driven out by natural disasters, sometimes I was driven out by rude people. Many times it was centered around my furry traveling companion. I believe there are really only two types of people, those who love animals and those who don't. When people see me walking my beautiful, sweet, elderly dog, they either come up and pet her, or they say something harsh.

One incident was a woman, a total stranger, who came up to me smiling down at Sadie and asked how old she was. I replied, "She is 13 and a half years old." The woman replied very curtly "She needs to be put down." Sadie was walking around, alert, and happy, and yet this woman wanted me to end her life because she was old.

Speaking of animals, several times I came very close to driving into an animal on the road. I can't stress enough how many times this will happen to you, and all I can say is, be alert at all times while you are driving. When you travel a lot of miles, you will get tired, so stop and smell the roses, and try not to drive at night.

Good things that happened:

One of the sheer joys of taking a road trip is the unpredictability of it. You never know what you will see. I am originally from Oregon, and bears are not a common sight. So, while driving high up in the Blue Mountains, I looked over and saw a bear! So exciting! He didn't stay for long, kind of shy, but so cute. I love animals, so to see the rich and wonderful amount of wildlife in our country gladdened my heart.

I met many great people on my trip, from all walks of life. They were a walking, talking advertisement for our beautiful country. I smiled at them, and they smiled back. We are all Americans, and we are all part of the human race. When you meet people across the country, you realize just how important it is to get to know your fellow citizens, and learn more about how they view the world and our country.

I have to give a special shout-out to the many dedicated people, often volunteers, who staff our state and national parks and monuments. They work tirelessly to ensure the health of our natural resources, and help travelers enjoy their visit. The same is true of the many people who staff the museums in small towns and large cities. They enjoy history, like I do, and it shows in their smiles.

Along with wonderful people, I have seen an America that is spectacularly beautiful, with open prairies, majestic mountains, and crystal clear rivers. I have seen a small fraction of the history of our country. I have seen the memorials to the brave people who shaped our country. I have fallen in love with America in a way that was not possible sitting in my living room. People ask me, "would I do it again?" The answer comes easily, "Yes, in a heartbeat."

Bibliography and Further Reading

B alfour, Amy C. *Southwest USA's Best Trips: 32 Amazing Road Trips*. Lonely Planet, 2014.

Boothill Graveyard, Boothill Graveyard

Chino, Conroy. *Petroglyphs of the Southwest: a Puebloan Perspective*. Western National Parks Association, 2012.

Corbett, Christopher. *Orphans Preferred: the Twisted Truth and Lasting Legend of the Pony Express*. Broadway Books, 2004.

Diamond, Jared M. *Collapse: How Societies Choose to Fail or Succeed*. Penguin Books, 2011.

Enss, Chris. *Tales behind the Tombstones*. Morris Pub., 2007.

Finch, etc. al.., Jackie. *Eyewitness Travel USA*. DK Publishing, 2017.

Fort Churchill, Nevada State Parks

Krause, Mariella. *Southwest USA's Best Trips: 32 Amazing Trips*. Lonely Planet, 2014.

Noble, David Grant. *Ancient Ruins and Rock Art of the Southwest: an Archaeological Guide*. Taylor Trade Publishing, 2015.

Noble, David Grant. *Ancient Ruins of the Southwest: an Archaeological Guide*. Northland Pub., 2000.

Oberding, Janice. *Haunted Nevada: Ghosts and Strange Phenomena of the Silver State*. Stackpole Books, 2013.

Oberding, Janice. *Haunted Virginia City*. Haunted America, a Division of the History Press, 2015.

Take My Hand, Walk with Me, Comstock Cemetery Foundation

Varney, Philip. *Ghost Towns of the Mountain West: Your Guide to the Hidden History and Old West Haunts of Colorado, Wyoming, Idaho, Montana, Utah, and Nevada*. MBI Pub. Co. and Voyageur Press, 2010.

Index

Referenced by Sections

About the Author

Julie Bettendorf is a world traveler with a degree in archaeology and a background in history. She has traveled extensively throughout Egypt, Central America, South America, Europe, and the United Kingdom, visiting archaeological and historical sites all along the way.

Currently, Julie is traveling around the US visiting ghost towns, ancient rock art sites, and archaeological wonders as part of research for her ongoing historical travel series entitled ***Wandering Woman***. Wandering Woman is a set of state-by-state guides, full of photographs, historical anecdotes, and unique tips to help other women travel and explore solo across the US by car. Julie enjoys writing freelance blogs, traveling frequently with her two adult children, and hiking outdoors with her faithful dog companion Rosie.

Also By Julie Bettendorf

Wandering Woman: Nevada is the third book in the **Wandering Woman Travel Series**. The first two books **Wandering Woman: Montana**, and **Wandering Woman: Utah** are available in ebook and paperback.

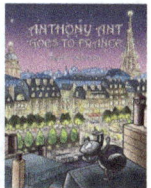

Julie has published two children's books in an ongoing, beautifully illustrated travel series entitled ***Anthony Ant Goes to France*** and ***Anthony Ant Goes to Egypt***.

She has also published a work of historical fiction entitled ***Luxor: Book of Past Lives*** which has recently been released as an audiobook, read by renowned narrator Barry Shannon.